Mr Men-a first reading adventure

PRICE STERN SLOAN LIMITED, NORTHAMPTON, ENGLAND

The fun way to bring learning to life

This book is part of the **Questron** system, which offers children a unique aid to learning and endless hours of challenging entertainment.

The **Questron** Electronic Answer Wand uses a microchip to sense correct and incorrect answers with "right" or "wrong" sounds and lights. Victory sounds and lights reward the user when particular sets of questions or games are completed. Powered by a nine-volt alkaline battery, which is activated only when the wand is pressed on a page, **Questron** should have an exceptionally long life. The **Questron** Electronic Answer Wand can be used with any book in the **Questron** series.

A note to parents...

With **Questron**, right or wrong answers are indicated instantly and can be tried over and over again to reinforce learning and improve skills. Children need not be restricted to the books designated for their age group, as interests and rates of development vary widely. Also, within many of the books, certain pages are designed for the older end of the age group and will provide a stimulating challenge to younger children.

Many activities are designed at different levels. For example, the child can select an answer by recognizing a letter or by reading an entire word. The activities for pre-readers and early readers are intended to be used with parental assistance. Interaction with parents or older children will stimulate the learning experience.

Printed in Great Britain by
Purnell Book Production Limited
Member of the BPCC Group

How to start Questron®

Hold **Questron**
at this angle and press the
activator button firmly on the page.

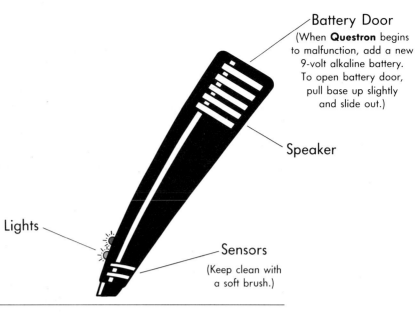

Battery Door
(When **Questron** begins
to malfunction, add a new
9-volt alkaline battery.
To open battery door,
pull base up slightly
and slide out.)

Speaker

Lights

Sensors
(Keep clean with
a soft brush.)

How to use Questron®

Press

Press **Questron** firmly on
the shape below, then lift it off.

Track

Press **Questron** down on ''Start'' and keep it
pressed down as you move to ''Finish''.

Start

Finish

Right and wrong with Questron®

Press **Questron**
on the square.

See the green light and
hear the sound. This
green light and sound
say ''You are correct''.

Press **Questron**
on the triangle.

The red light and sound
say ''Try again''. Lift
Questron off the page and
wait for the sound to stop.

Press **Questron**
on the circle.

Hear the victory sound.
Don't be dazzled
by the flashing lights.
You deserve them.

Mr. Sleepy

Mr. Lazy

Mr. Rush

Mr. Messy

Mr. Slow

Mr. Glad

Mr. Sneeze

Mr. Bounce

Mr. Grumpy

Mr. Funny

Mr. Healthy

Mr. Impossible

Mr. Skinny

Mr. Tall

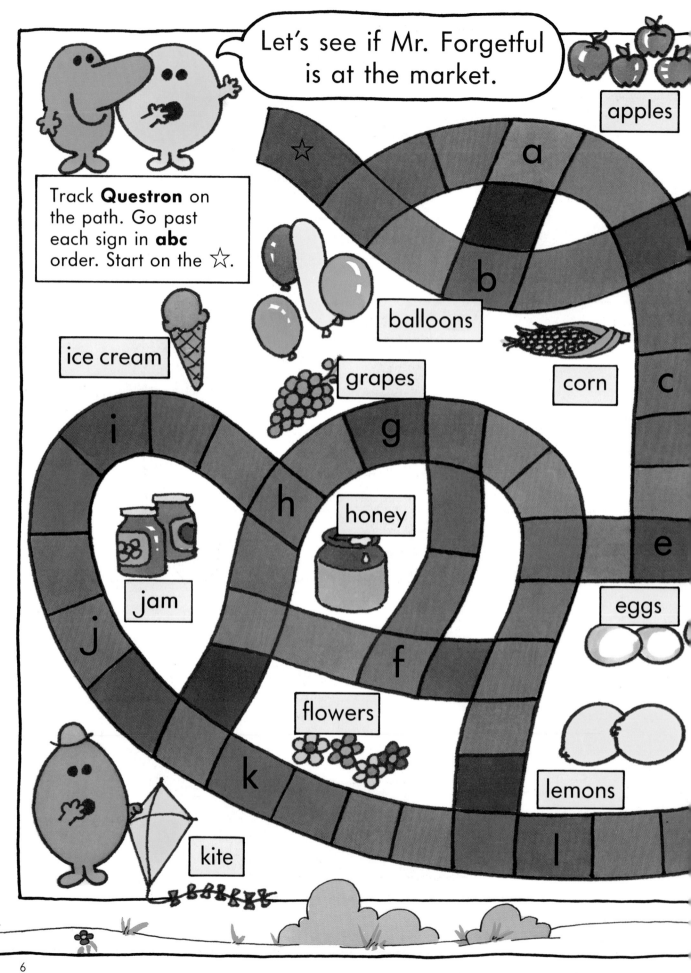

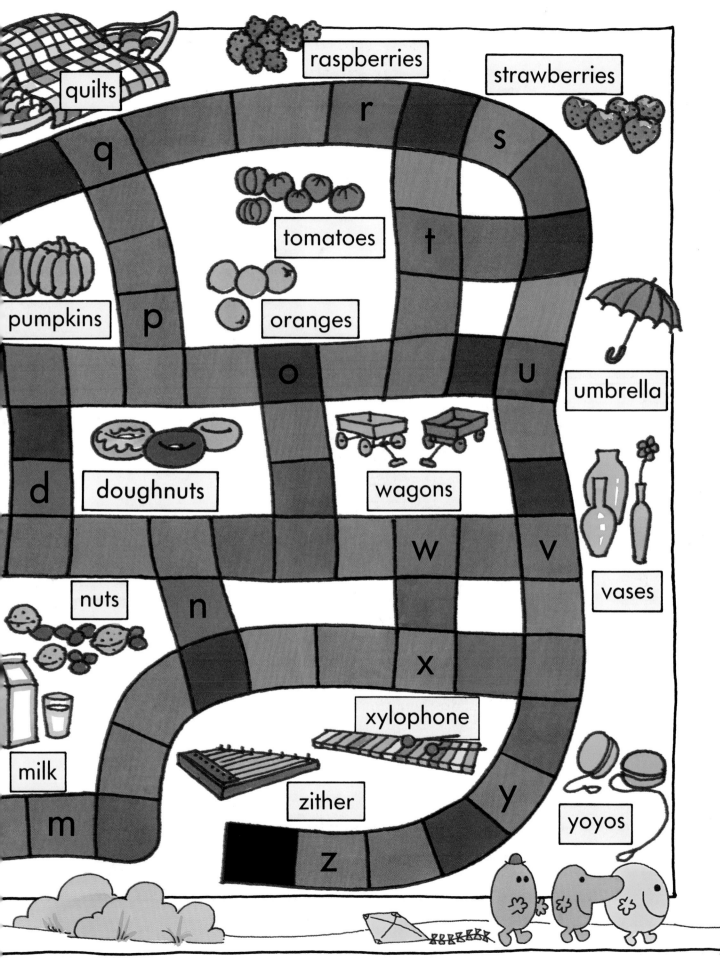

quilts

raspberries

strawberries

q

r

s

tomatoes

t

pumpkins

p

oranges

o

u

umbrella

d

doughnuts

wagons

w

v

vases

nuts

n

x

xylophone

milk

zither

y

yoyos

m

z

Good news! We found Mr. Grumpy at the rodeo.

Press **Questron** on the correct colour word in each sentence about the rodeo.

The horse is | brown |
| blue |
.

The flag is | red |
| blue |
.

The hat is | purple |
| red |
.

The rope is | pink |
| white |
.

The fence is | black |
| green |
.

The calf is | yellow |
| pink |
.

green

blue

_ed

orange

white

_ellow

Press **Questron** on the letter that is missing from each colour word.

__lue

| b | w | d |

__ellow

| p | r | y |

__range

| t | o | c |

re__

| d | b | g |

whit__

| s | t | e |

gree__

| l | n | h |

9

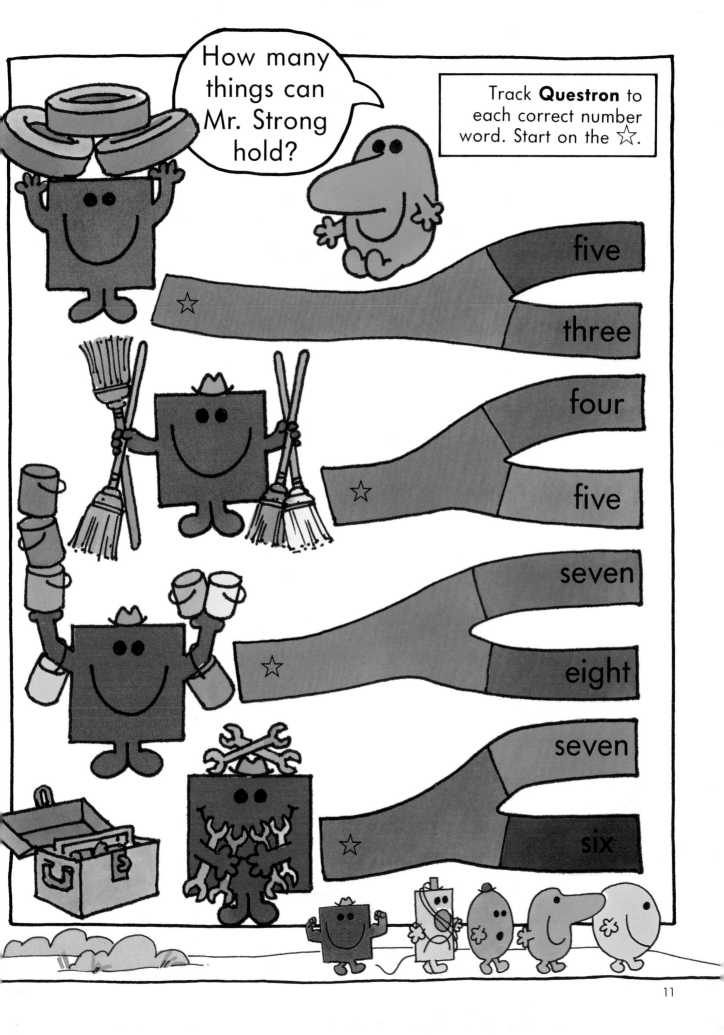

on

off

small

small

on

big

big

off

up

down

sit

sit

stand

stand

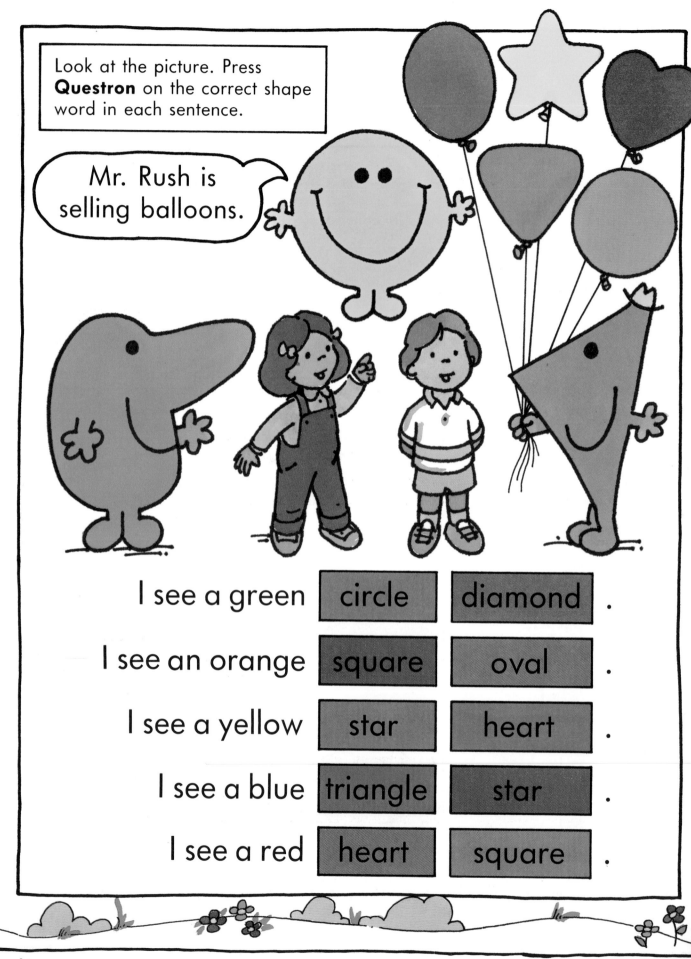

Look at the picture. Press **Questron** on the correct shape word in each sentence.

Mr. Rush is selling balloons.

I see a green | circle | diamond | .

I see an orange | square | oval | .

I see a yellow | star | heart | .

I see a blue | triangle | star | .

I see a red | heart | square | .

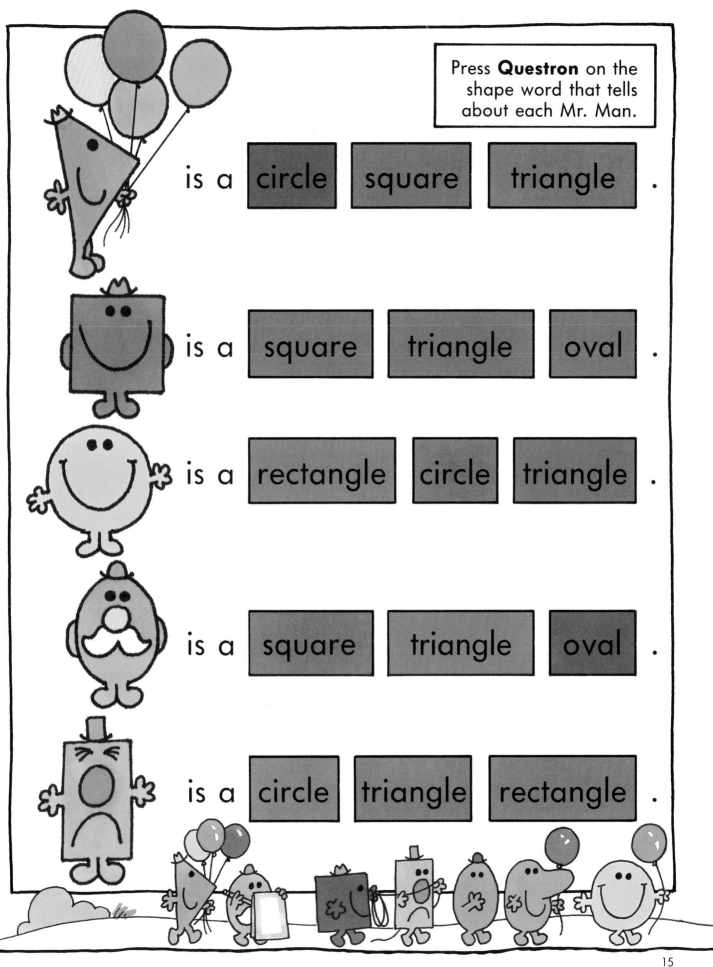

is a circle   square   triangle .

is a square   triangle   oval .

is a rectangle   circle   triangle .

is a square   triangle   oval .

is a circle   triangle   rectangle .

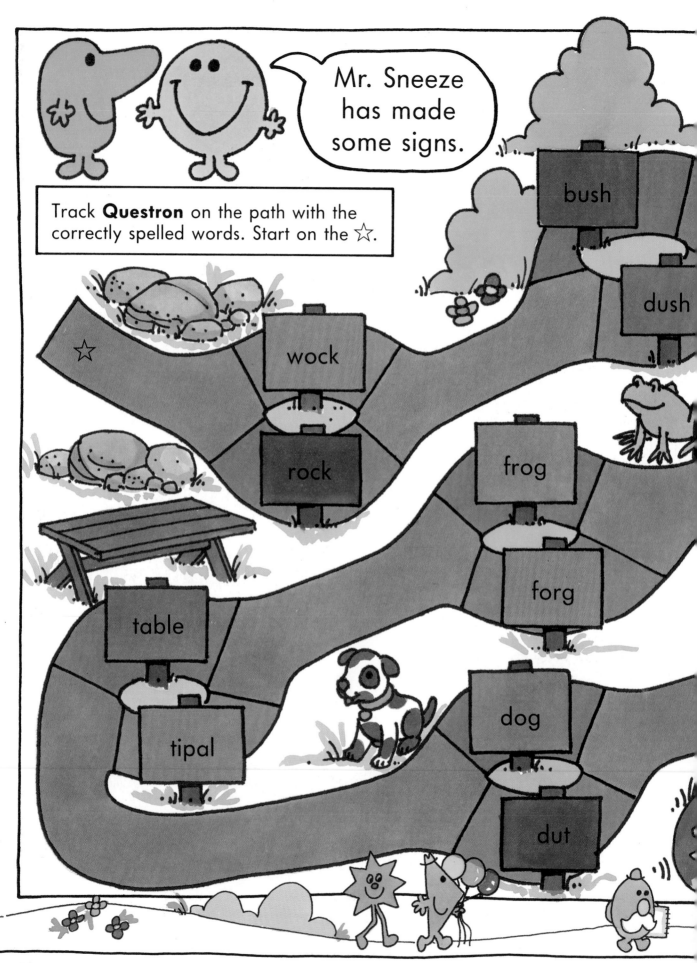

16

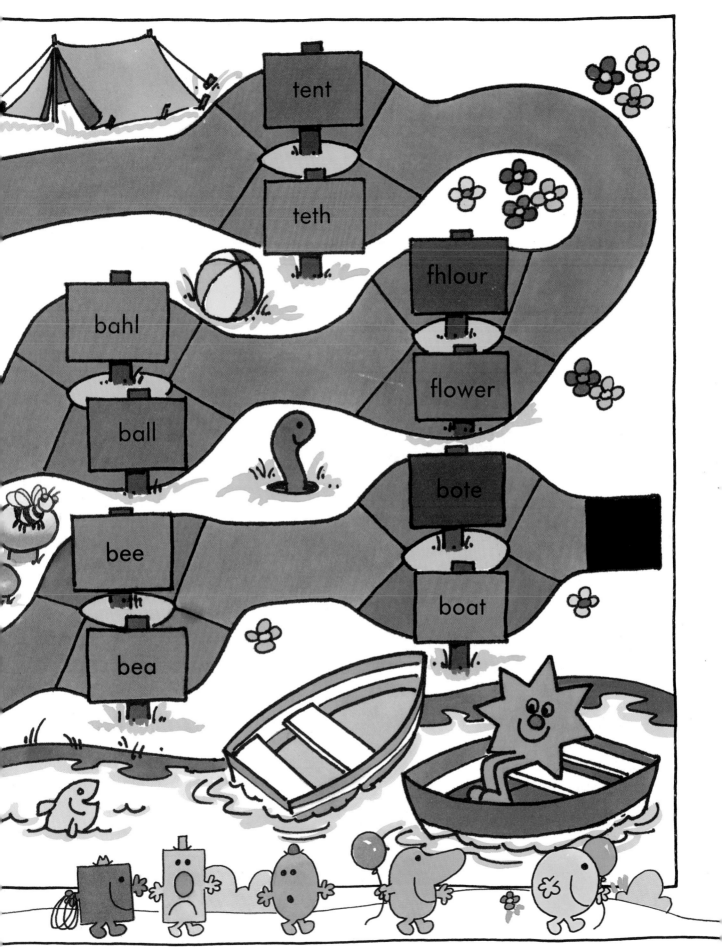

Read each sentence. Press **Questron** on the word in the boat that rhymes with the last word in each sentence.

fish

dog

sock

Mr. Happy is on the **dock**.

rake

ball

girl

Mr. Strong likes the **lake**.

goat

See you at the party!

cup

toy

Mr. Nosey looks in the **boat**.

Is Mr. Lazy too lazy to come to the party?

Look at each picture. Press **Questron** on the word that tells what Mr. Lazy is doing.

Mr. Lazy sleeps dances . all DAY.

Mr. Lazy writes reads a book.

Mr. Lazy throws eats an apple.

Mr. Lazy sits jumps on a blanket.

Read each sentence. Press **Questron** on each sentence below that is the same.

A goat runs on the hill.

A goat runs on the hill.

The goat has horns.

I see a cloud.

A cloud is in the sky.

I see a cloud.

Mr. Happy sees Mr. Skinny.

Mr. Skinny is yellow.

Mr. Happy sees Mr. Skinny.

The sky is blue.

I see the sky.

The sky is blue.

Press **Questron** on the six sentences that tell about the picture.

The flower is orange.   There are three plates.

A rock is under the tree.   The basket is yellow.

The blanket is purple.   The ball is on the snow.

A flower is under the tree.   The cups are blue.

The blanket has stars.   A plane flies above.

Go **under** me.

Go **behind** me.

Go **around** me.

Go **in front** of me.

Read each sentence about the desert maze. Press **Questron** on the word that correctly completes each sentence.

The buzzards are green brown .

The Mr. Men see a cat spider .

The cactus has red blue flowers.

There are two three camels.

The wheel is bigger smaller than Mr. Small.

The snake is on the table rocks .

What hat does the nurse have?

☆		She	has	does	.
		hat	the	baseball	.
		tall	blue	cap	.

How many hats is Mr. Nosey wearing?

☆		Mr.	Nosey	cats	.
		does	has	two	.
		three	four	hats	.

Who has the chef's hat?

☆		The	socks	ribbon	.
		sailor	cup	hat	.
		wears	the	chef's	.

It's time to go to Mr. Silly's party.

Come on, Mr. Tall and Mr. Impossible!

Look at the houses in Mr. Silly's street. Read the sentences. Press **Questron** on the sentences that tell about the houses.

Mr. Funny's house is shorter than the green house.

There are eight square houses.

Mr. Impossible's house is upside down.

Mr. Small's house has a blue roof.

Mr. Impossible's house has a broken door.

The purple house belongs to Mr. Skinny.

Mr. Silly's house is bigger than Mr. Small's.

Mr. Small's house has three windows.

Mr. Tall's house is the green house.

Mr. Silly's house is next to Mr. Skinny's house.

Now all the Mr. Men are here! What a silly party!

Track **Questron** through the mazes to read the silly sentences about the silly party. Start on the ☆.

☆	The	cake	looks	.
	candle	has	flowers	.

☆	Some	hats	happy	cones	.
	horns	are	ice	cream	.
	cold	shoes	blow	sweet	.

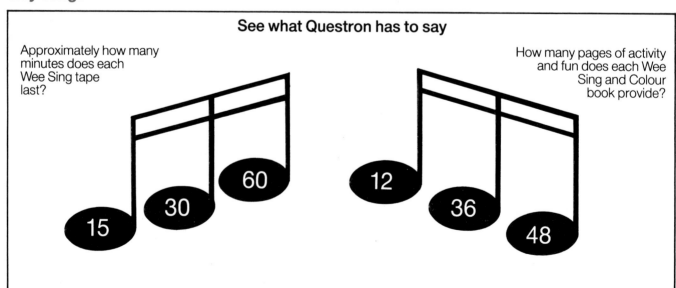